This
Ostara Journal
Belongs To:

_____

Around March 21st – Northern Hemisphere
Around September 23rd – Southern Hemisphere

Thanks for buying this journal!
I have lots more available on Amazon, including:

- Journals
- Undated Planners
- Composition Books (for school)
- Holiday themes
- Mermaids, Seahorses, starfish (I live near the beach, constant theme!)
- Florals & botanicals
- Hobby-themed journals for gardening, yoga, chakra-balancing, and other self-improvement topics – and some witchy stuff!

I'm Wanda, and Moon Magic Soul is my brand – welcome to my tribe!

Visit me:

www.moonmagicsoul.com

www.facebook.com/moonmagisoul

Using this Journal/Workbook

Welcome to the Season of Ostara!

The pages are a way for you to explore and celebrate the season – to document your thoughts and feelings about Ostara, and also to reflect on the past year, and keep moving through the new year!

Fill out what speaks to you – what you'd like to express. Ignore what doesn't fire you or interest you.

The first few pages are some month and week pages for personal planning. There are two months and six weeks – which gets you from Imbolc to just past Ostara. If you already have a personal planner, you can art journal or ignore those pages.

Journaling – there are lots of journal prompts, have some fun with it! There are also some blank pages for you to doodle, scrapbook (paste or glue things) or make plans without lined pages.

Blessed be!

Sunday	Monday	Tuesday	Wednesday
☐	☐	☐	☐
☐	☐	☐	☐
☐	☐	☐	☐
☐	☐	☐	☐
☐	☐	☐	☐

Thursday	Friday	Saturday	

Sunday	Monday	Tuesday	Wednesday

MONTH

Thursday	Friday	Saturday

WEEK OF:

_____

Monday

Tuesday

Wednesday

Thursday

Friday

Saturday

Sunday

Notes

WEEK OF:

_____

Monday

Tuesday

Wednesday

Thursday

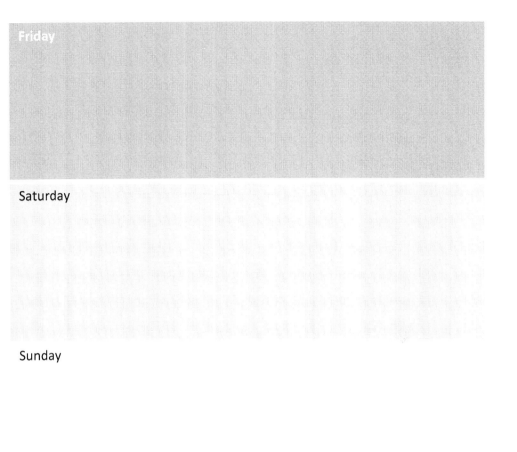

Friday

Saturday

Sunday

Notes

WEEK OF:

Monday

Tuesday

Wednesday

Thursday

Friday

Saturday

Sunday

Notes

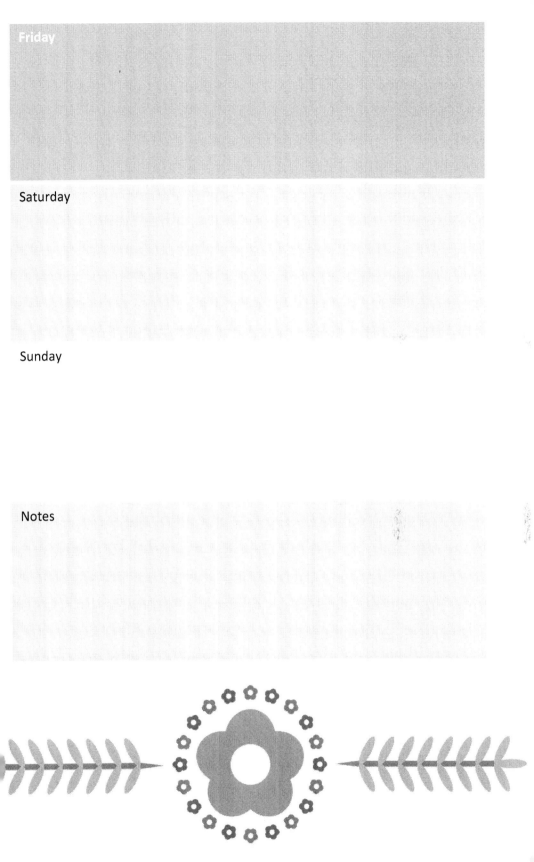

WEEK OF:

Monday

Tuesday

Wednesday

Thursday

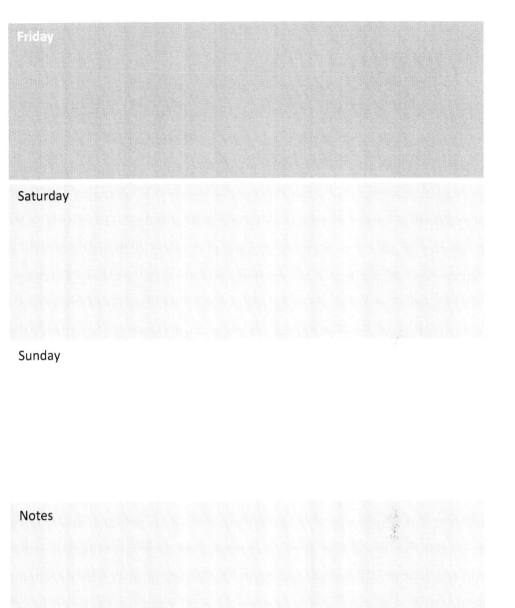

Friday

Saturday

Sunday

Notes

WEEK OF:

_____

Monday

Tuesday

Wednesday

Thursday

Friday

Saturday

Sunday

Notes

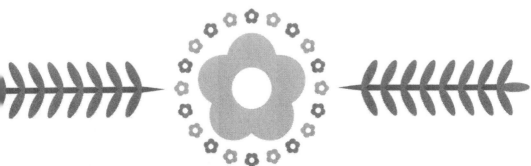

WEEK OF:

Monday

Tuesday

Wednesday

Thursday

Friday

Saturday

Sunday

Notes

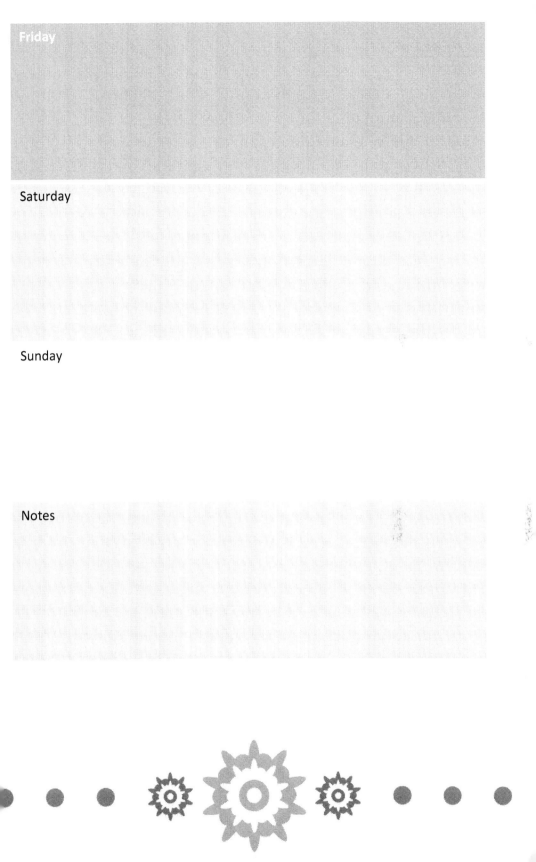

Meaning & Keywords

- ❑ Beginnings, awakening and renewal
- ❑ Cleansing/cleaning
- ❑ Sprouting seeds
- ❑ Fertility
- ❑ Transitions and changes

After celebrating Yule and Imbolc, this is the season where the intentions set at the beginning of the year begin to grow – and maybe even blossom!

Continue the cleaning that you began during Imbolc, and plant seeds of health, wealth and happiness! Get outside and thank the goddess for this beautiful world, and shed your light on others!

How have you celebrated during the warming season since Imbolc?

_____

_____

_____

_____

_____

_____

_____

_____

_____

_____

_____

_____

_____

_____

_____

_____

_____

_____

_____

_____

_____

How has your life changed since last Ostara?

What have you planted in your mind and your life?

How are your intentions growing and blossoming?

Have you planned or planted a spring garden yet?

Scents of the Season

- ❑ Ginger
- ❑ Sage
- ❑ Lavender
- ❑ Thyme
- ❑ Rose
- ❑ Geranium

Scenting Your Home

- ❑ Incense
- ❑ Candles
- ❑ Essential Oils with Scent Sticks
- ❑ Essential Oils in Diffusers
- ❑ Essential Oils rubbed on air vents
- ❑ Commercial plugs (no judgment)

What scents make you think of the spring time?

How do you plan to use scent this season?

_____

_____

_____

_____

_____

_____

_____

_____

_____

_____

_____

_____

_____

_____

_____

_____

_____

_____

_____

Horn of Plenty Oil Recipe

Here's a great recipe for Horn of Plenty Oil, which is listed later in this book as a ritual activity

Mandarin orange essential oil -5 drops
Lemon essential oil – 5 drops
Strawberry essential oil – 5 drops
Blackberry essential oil – 5 drops
Ginger essential oil – 5 drops
Tobacco (pinch)
Kernel of dried corn
Grapeseed oil – just under 1 ounce

Mix up in a small glass bottle and seal tightly. Discard when oil smells rancid and mix up a new batch.

Use to anoint doorways and candles, and to write sigils on skin!

Decorations

- ☐ Colors – white, green, pastel colors of pink, aqua and purple
- ☐ Rabbits and bunnies
- ☐ Birds – especially robins and chicks
- ☐ Baskets (with flowers and decorated eggs)
- ☐ All spring flowers – violets, crocus, daffodil, tulip, jasmine, rose, iris, peony

Do you decorate the entrance to your home to welcome the coming spring?

_____

_____

_____

Do you decorate the living space of your home for spring?

_____

_____

_____

What decorations are you seeing when you go out?

Have you completed your spring cleaning from the Imbolc season? If not, list how you get that done!

_____

_____

_____

_____

_____

_____

_____

_____

_____

_____

_____

_____

_____

_____

_____

_____

_____

_____

_____

_____

_____

Foods

- ❑ Spring greens & herbs – asparagus and salads
- ❑ Eggs and egg recipes, like custards and quiches
- ❑ Edible flowers
- ❑ Honey cakes and hot crossed buns
- ❑ Violet jelly
- ❑ Strawberries
- ❑ Chocolate & chocolate candies
- ❑ Wine

Do you grow any food or herbs in your kitchen garden?

_____

_____

_____

Have you tried eating edible flowers?

_____

_____

_____

Find a recipe for Hot Crossed Buns and write it down!

What egg recipes do you like?

Ostara "Mean" Eggs

When my children were young, they loved the spring season – especially when I made "mean" eggs! The story – traditionally they are called "devilled" eggs, and they didn't like that the eggs were from a devil. So they compromised and called them "mean" instead!

Ingredients:

6 eggs
2 Tbsp. mayonnaise
2 teaspoons Dijon mustard
Salt and pepper to taste
1 tablespoon fresh chopped dill weed or 1 teaspoon dried
Paprika

1) Boil eggs and allow to cool. Peel, and slice lengthwise. Remove yolks to a small bowl, placing the whites on a nice plate.
2) Using a fork, mash the egg yolks. Add in mayonnaise, mustard, dill, salt and pepper and dill, mixing well.
3) Carefully spoon or pipe the yolk mixture into the egg white cups, and sprinkle with paprika. Chill before serving.

Look up and list what flowers are edible!

What are your favorite spring vegetables?

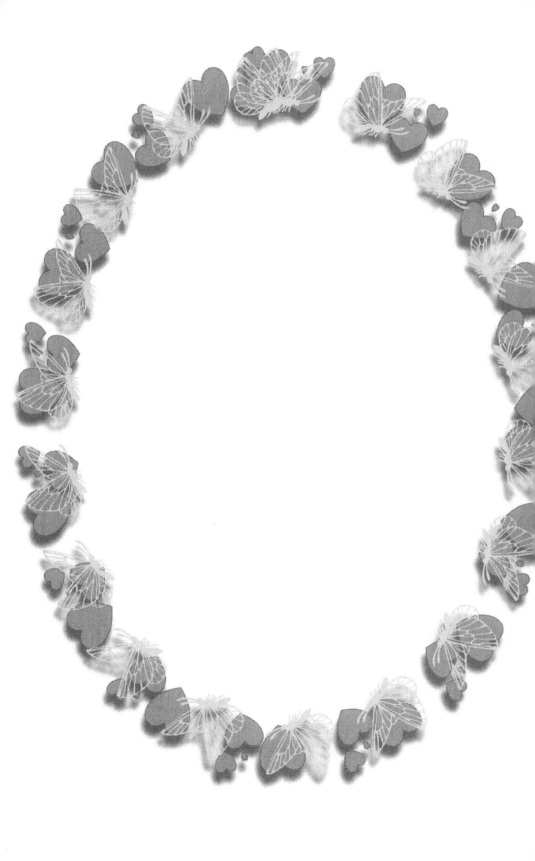

Activities for Ostara

- ☐ Set up your altar – bring in elements of spring with flowers and decorated eggs
- ☐ Take a walk and notice the birds, the air, the animals
- ☐ Meditate outside – listen to the goddess
- ☐ Plant something! Use crushed eggshells as a fertilizer
- ☐ Make hot cross buns
- ☐ Lay under a tree and enjoy the spring
- ☐ Watch birds in a quiet park, or make a bird feeder
- ☐ Pick flowers (and thank the earth)
- ☐ Have a picnic with Ostara foods
- ☐ Dye eggs
- ☐ Collect stones, feathers and flowers for your altar

What items are you using to decorate your altar?

How often do you re-decorate your altar?

Sketch a new plan for your altar setup here:

What quadrant of your altar is good for flowers?

On your Ostara walk – list what all you noticed!

List the most notable moments that birds have gifted you with their feathers:

_____

_____

_____

_____

_____

_____

_____

_____

_____

_____

_____

_____

_____

_____

_____

_____

_____

_____

_____

_____

_____

_____

_____

How often do you meditate? Have you tried any new meditation methods lately?

_____

_____

_____

_____

_____

_____

_____

_____

_____

_____

_____

_____

_____

_____

_____

_____

_____

_____

_____

_____

_____

_____

_____

Deities for Ostara

- Eostre
- The Maiden
- Astarte
- Aurora
- Kore
- Persephone
- Venus
- Aphrodite
- Narcissus
- Freya
- Isis
- Dionysus
- Apollo

Do you have a particular deity that you work with during the spring season?

How do you honor and thank the gods for the renewal of spring?

How often do you smudge yourself – and your home?

Look up information about a deity you haven't met yet and write down what you find:

How are you planning to celebrate the Ostara season?

Spellwork & Rituals:

- ☐ Make an egg charm – blow out the yolk, decorate the shell, and make an enchantment to manifest your desires
- ☐ Wash your front door with water and anoint with Horn of Plenty oil or spearmint to welcome in wealth
- ☐ Work candle spells for clarity and renewal
- ☐ Leave crushed eggshells as an offering on your altar, and later tuck those into a bush or flower bed outside your home
- ☐ Make a ritual of planting seeds to manifest new beginnings and wealth. Move the seedlings near a window or outside as weather allows

List intentions that you set at Samhain and Yuletide. What are you contributing to manifest these intentions?

How have you honoured the Mother Goddess with new growth in your life this year?

Do you have a social group that you can celebrate the sabbats and esbats with? Why or why not?

_____

_____

_____

_____

_____

_____

_____

_____

_____

_____

_____

_____

_____

_____

_____

_____

_____

_____

_____

_____

_____

Do you have a daily witchy practice to keep you in tune with the universe? List here – if not, develop one!

_____

_____

_____

_____

_____

_____

_____

_____

_____

_____

_____

_____

_____

_____

_____

_____

_____

_____

_____

What are your favorite divination tools? Why?

Divination –
Looking Forward:

The next pages are spaces for you to record by month what your favorite divination tools are telling you about your upcoming year.

Make it a habit to review your reading on a monthly basis, and make comments about what has unfolded. Leave space in between for future journaling and exploration!

Month 1
The Season of Ostara

Month 1
Reflections

Month 2
The Season of Beltane

Month 2
Reflections

Month 3
The Season of Litha

Month 3
Reflections

Month 4
The Season of Summer

Month 4
Reflections

Month 5
The Season of Lammas

Month 5
Reflections

Month 6
The Season of Late Summer

Month 6
Reflections

Month 7
The Season of Samhain

Month 7
Reflections

Month 8
The Year Begins

Month 8
Reflections

Month 9
The Season of Yule

Month 9
Reflections

Month 10
The Season of Winter

Month 10
Reflections

Month 11
The Season of Imbolc

Month 11
Reflections

Month 12
The Season of Spring

Month 12
Reflections

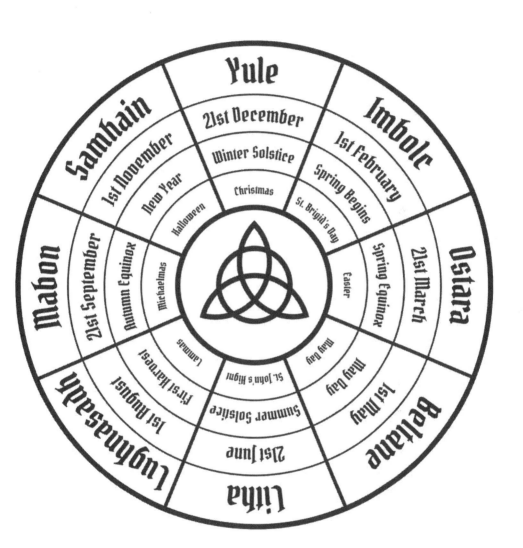

Thanks for buying this journal!
I have lots more available on Amazon, including:

- Journals
- Undated Planners
- Composition Books (for school)
- Holiday themes
- Mermaids, Seahorses, starfish (I live near the beach, constant theme!)
- Florals & botanicals
- Hobby-themed journals for gardening, yoga, chakra-balancing, and other self-improvement topics – and some witchy stuff!

I'm Wanda, and Moon Magic Soul is my brand – welcome to my tribe!

Visit me:

www.moonmagicsoul.com

www.facebook.com/moonmagisoul

Printed in Great Britain
by Amazon

76936488R00061